D1716359

J577.64 D   1/18
SM

Seasons of the
Estuary Biome

Written by
Shirley Duke

rourkeeducationalmedia.com

www.rourkeeducationalmedia.com

PHOTO CREDITS: Cover: svetlana foote; Title Page © Isantilli; Page 4 © Masonjar, PixelEmbargo; Page 5 © AridOcean; Page 6 © Sherry Yates Young; Page 7 © Snapper 68; Page 8 © Arun Roisri; Page 9 © George Chernilevsky; Page 10 © Vladimir Melnikov; Page 11 © Lori Skelton; Page 12 © NOAA; Page 13 © worldswildlifewonders; Page 14 © Zereshk; Page 15 © Vitaliy Urazov; Page 15 A © Lori Skelton; Page 16 © Nonnakrit; Page 17 © Matthew Connolly and Ye Choh Wah; Page 18 © Mario Savoia; Page 19 © Kishano; Page 20 Joel M. Galloway , USGS; Page 21 © Vladislav Gajic and PixelEmbargo;

Edited by Jill Sherman

Cover design by Renee Brady
Interior design by Nicola Stratford bdpublishing.com

Library of Congress PCN Data

Seasons of the Estuary Biome / Shirley Duke
(Biomes)
ISBN 978-1-62169-893-7 (hard cover)
ISBN 978-1-62169-788-6 (soft cover)
ISBN 978-1-62717-000-0 (e-Book)
Library of Congress Control Number: 2013936809

Rourke Educational Media
Printed in the United States of America,
North Mankato, Minnesota

rourkeeducationalmedia.com
customerservice@rourkeeducationalmedia.com • PO Box 643328 Vero Beach, Florida 32964

Table of Contents

Fresh and Salty

Rivers flow to the sea and spill freshwater into the salty seawater.

These are estuaries, where freshwater and **salt** water meet.

Estuaries have:

✓ Salt water and freshwater
✓ Grasses and seaweed
✓ Seasons like the nearby land
✓ Nesting grounds for young animals

Otter

Estuaries are where rivers meet the sea. Estuaries can be found along the coast.

4

The amount of salt in an estuary changes all the time.

Water moves in and out. Storms and **tides** change the mix.

Estuaries are homes for many kinds of life. Eggs hatch in estuaries. Tiny fish hide in the grasses. Baby shrimp swim and grow. Shore and water birds stop to rest.

Snowy Egret

Salt marshes, mangrove forests, mud flats, rocky intertidal shores, reefs, and barrier beaches may be part of an estuary.

Estuaries help clean the moving water. Estuaries **filter** water and protect the shore from storm waves.

Mangrove Forest

7

Salt Water Changes

Estuary seasons follow the seasons of the nearby land.

In the winter, many of the **creatures** in estuaries lay eggs. The water in the estuaries is warmer than in the open seas, which keeps the eggs safe.

Crabs carry their eggs on their bodies. Most other animals let their eggs float in the water.

Spring often brings rain. Rivers flood, spilling freshwater into the estuaries and seas.

When rivers flood more freshwater goes into the estuaries making the water less salty.

Many birds build their nests in estuaries. Other birds stop in estuaries to rest and eat as they fly north in the spring.

In summer, big storms toss salt water inland and it spills into estuaries. The water in the estuary now has more salt.

Bar-built estuaries are protected by sandbars or barrier islands.

Young animals grow up during the summer. Plants grow and make food in the Sun.

By the end of the summer the otter offspring look like their parents.

In the fall, some young leave the estuary. Others stay behind.

Many sea animals spend part of their life cycle in estuaries.

The cycle of seasons begins again with winter soon on its way.

Saltwater Marsh

A Great Blue Heron fishing in an estuary.

Life in an Estuary

Estuary plants offer animals food and a place to hide.

When plants die and **decompose**, this makes food for other animals.

Exposed roots make a good hiding place for animals.

Water flows into estuaries bringing with it tasty worms, fish, and **shellfish**.

Small fish **dart** between the grasses under the water. They nibble and then hide from birds, blue crabs, turtles, and snails.

Once prawns reach maturity, they leave the estuaries and head for the ocean.

Seagulls may catch prey in estuaries.

Future of Estuaries

Many big cities sit near estuaries. People use estuaries to make their living.

New York City is built on an estuary.

Too many people can harm estuaries. They want land to live on, so they drain the water.

Too many fish are caught for food. Trash often ends up in estuaries.

People build dams. The water changes its path. Young fish and shellfish have no place to lay eggs.

We can protect estuaries from harm. Work to restore estuaries and keep them safe. Estuaries are important to all life.

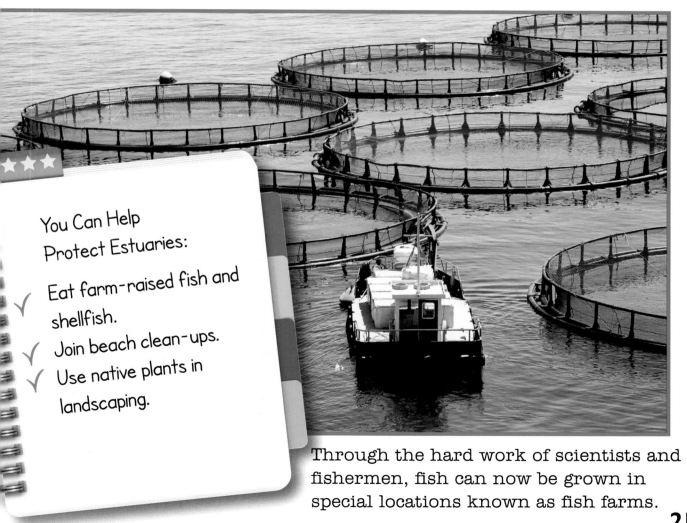

You Can Help
Protect Estuaries:

✓ Eat farm-raised fish and shellfish.
✓ Join beach clean-ups.
✓ Use native plants in landscaping.

Through the hard work of scientists and fishermen, fish can now be grown in special locations known as fish farms.

Study Like a Scientist
Reduce the Salt

How does water becomes less salty?

1. Fill a cup halfway with water and add 2 spoons of salt. Stir and taste.

2. Now, fill the cup to the top and taste it again.

Adding more water makes it less salty. This is what happens when a flooded river empties into an estuary making the water have a lower salt content.

Glossary

creatures (KREE-churz): animals and other living things

dart (DAHRT): to move quickly

decompose (dee-kuhm-POZE): to rot or decay and break down

filter (FIL-tur): to clean or strain as a liquid passes through

salt (SAWLT): a common white substance in sea water

shellfish (SHEL-fish): a soft-bodied animal with a shell, such as a clam, mussel, or crab

tides (TIDEZ): the regular changes in the level of the sea caused by the moon's pull of gravity

young (YUHNG): a baby or offspring

Index

Websites

water.epa.gov/learn/kids/estuaries/index.cfm

games.noaa.gov

kids.nceas.ucsb.edu/biomes/estuaries.html

About the Author

Shirley Duke has enjoyed science all of her life. She has written many books about science. She lives in Texas and New Mexico and loves the different seasons in each place. She has explored estuaries along the Texas coast and tasted oysters many times.

Meet The Author!
www.meetREMauthors.com